MORE THAN THE SCORE

Life Lessons Through Sports

By
Chris Givens

First published by Dog Ear Publishing
4010 W. 86th Street, Ste H
Indianapolis, IN 46268
www.dogearpublishing.net

ISBN: 978-159858-819-4

This book is printed on acid-free paper.

Printed in the United States of America

INTRODUCTION

Growing up in a large family, with three younger brothers and an older sister, there was always plenty of healthy competition to be had. Before I ever pulled on my first official team jersey I had become used to a daily dose of competition with my siblings. My Dad was a firm believer in the power of competition and the value it brought in terms of teaching life lessons He was a huge sports fan and sports and the outdoors were a very big part of our lives.

My Dad was competitive and I know he always wanted me and my various sports teams to be successful. However, at the same time, he never seemed to be as concerned about whether I won or lost as he was about what I learned in the process. He never missed the opportunity to take a competitive situation and turn it into a lesson that could be used in daily life. This book is a tribute to my Dad and all that I've learned from him. Thanks for the lessons and for always being my number one fan. I miss you dearly.

Lesson #1: What Comes Around Goes Around

Recess in third grade meant one thing and one thing only – marbles!! There were kid-made marble holes all over the playground. It got to be so big that playing marbles only at recess just wasn't enough. Soon each house in the neighborhood had these same marble holes and we'd play from dinner time until the streetlights came on.

I used an empty oatmeal container to hold my most prized marbles, the "jumbos." My best friend, Stu, and I didn't like to mess around with the small marbles so we'd play almost exclusively for jumbos. Two at a time, three at a time, four…whatever. Stu was kind of known as the neighborhood ace and I do admit he was pretty good. On one particular evening I had called him to come over and play marbles after dinner. While waiting for him to come screaming through our back yard on his bike, I decided to take a quick inventory. Recess had proven to be quite lucrative in the jumbo category over the past few days and I was proud of my current stock of 56 jumbos.

Stu soon arrived and we began our friendly dual. I'd win a match here and there, but overall I was getting destroyed. I could feel the oatmeal container getting lighter and lighter each time I went back to fill my pockets with jumbos. Stu knew he had me on a bad night and kept upping the ante.

"Each guy plays three this time," he'd say.

I knew it wasn't smart, but I'd go ahead and play anyway. Soon the streetlights came on and it was time for Stu to head home and for me to assess the damage. I sat down in the middle of our living room floor, dumped what was left in the oatmeal container, and stared down in disbelief. Slowly counting each jumbo one by one I came to the realization that what I sensed was happening was actually worse than I anticipated. My pre game count of 56 jumbos was now down to 16.

"Sixteen," I whispered softly to no one in particular. "I've only got sixteen left". With that, I started to cry and slowly returned each jumbo to the oatmeal container one by one. I was about half finished when Dad came into the living room from the kitchen.

"Got cleaned out tonight, huh?" he said with a smile.

With a smile. Why is he smiling? This is devastating to a third grader and he's smiling?

"Yeah, I did. Stu took almost all of them," I said trying to be audible with the choppy breath and "crying stutter" kids get when they're really upset.

"He *won* almost all of them, you mean?" Dad asked.

"Yeah, he won almost all of them," I replied as I dropped my sixteenth, and last, jumbo back into the oatmeal container.

"Well, you'll get another chance and next time it will be different. You will be in a situation where you've cleaned someone out, too, so remember the feeling now and do your best to not let it happen the next time," Dad said.

I didn't truly believe it at the time, but Dad was right. Stu and I played again and it was different. I don't know that I won all 40 of my jumbos back, but there were definitely days when he felt cleaned out.

A bad day today doesn't mean a bad day tomorrow. Learn from your setbacks and use them as motivation.

Lesson #2:   Be Willing To Make Sacrifices

I was really into Little League baseball from age eight to age 12. My favorite position was pitcher and I took great pride in being able to throw hard and throw "junk." At least I thought I could throw junk, even if most of the time my curveball didn't curve, my sinker didn't sink, and my changeup didn't change much from the pitch I threw before it. I enjoyed pitching and trying new grips, new pitches, and throwing fastballs as hard as I could.

There was one little problem, however, with my quest to be the most dominating Little League pitcher Houghton County had ever seen. I was afraid of hitting someone with a pitch. Many summer nights after dinner Dad would finish reading the paper then ask, "Do you want to throw?" Throw didn't mean just playing catch. It meant pitching and work-ing on perfecting my junk.

We'd head out to the alley behind our house, gloves in hand, and Dad would go through his standard routine of rub-bing the sole of his shoe in the dirt to mark the "mound" and then pacing off 46 feet. This was the Little League distance from the pitcher's rubber to home plate. Once the distance was marked, Dad would assume the catcher's position and say the same thing every time. "C'mon now. Throw hard. Don't aim it, just throw it."

Control, in terms of being able to throw the ball where I wanted to, wasn't exactly my forte at 12 years of age. I would take Dad's advice and throw hard, but I'd also throw high, low, way right, way left. You name a direction and I threw it there. Dad knew I didn't throw as hard as I could in games because of the fact that I was afraid of hitting someone and hurting them. His advice to me was always the same.

"Your job is to go out and pitch. Sometimes you're going to be a little wild, but it's also the batter's job to get out of the way. Don't feel like it's all your fault if you hit some-one. Everyone knows it's not on purpose and is just part of the game sometimes."

Even at 12, I could understand the reasoning, but it didn't help me feel any better about just going out and throwing hard instead of letting up and aiming the ball. Night after night we'd head to the alley and I would throw hard. That always meant several pitches in the dirt, which also meant several bouncing off Dad's shins, up into his stomach, and whizzing way over his head and well down the alley. Every time he'd get hit he would wince, rub it out, shake it off, and resume the position for more. Over time, I could see a steady improvement in my control. Fewer and fewer pitches were ending up in the dirt and the evidence was shown through fewer and fewer bruises and welts showing on Dad's legs. I ended up being a decent pitcher, but not even close to the best Houghton County had ever seen, although not the worst either.

Well after my Little League career was over I asked Dad why he put himself through that kind of pain, night after night, when it would have been much easier for him to just say, "Look Chris, you're just not meant to be a pitcher." He told me the reason he did it was because he knew it was going to be painful, but he also knew it would help me get over my fear of hitting someone in a game.

"I knew it bothered you when I got hit," he said. I also knew that if I just didn't make a big deal out of it, and kept you focused on throwing hard, that you'd end up doing the same thing when you pitched in the games".

Be willing to make sacrifices, even if they are painful, to help others reach their potential when maybe they don't see it in themselves.

Lesson #3: You Can Always Be A Kid At Heart

We often took family trips to Milwaukee, WI and Minneapolis, MN. Exactly where we were going and for how long depended on whether the Milwaukee Brewers or Minnesota Twins were playing at home and who their respective opponents were. If there was a chance for a double bonus, which meant also working in a Minnesota North Stars preseason home hockey game at the same time, then the decision was a no-brainer. We were going to Minneapolis.

While in Minneapolis we would always stay at the same hotel. It was very close to Metropolitan Stadium and the Metropolitan Sports Center which meant there was a very good chance the opposing teams would be staying there as well. One particular trip will always be my favorite.

We had just watched the Montreal Canadians play the North Stars the night before and I was barely awake when my Dad burst through the door.

"Chris, Chris, get up let's go!" my Dad said excitedly.

"Wait, what?, Go where? What's going on?" I asked, rubbing my eyes and squinting through what was my first light of the day.

"I went down to the restaurant to get a cup of coffee and all of the Montreal Canadians are down there!" he exclaimed. "Get a pen and some paper and let's go. Hurry."

He reached down for my arm and helped me up.

I quickly got dressed and followed my Dad toward the door. Once into the hallway my Dad turned and broke into what was almost a full sprint.

"Dad, wait for me," I said as I tried to run and keep from fumbling my pen and paper.

"Hurry," he answered. "They won't be there long."

I caught up to my Dad just before we made the final turn leading into the lobby and the restaurant entrance. He had slowed down and now we were walking side by side. I was only three or four strides into the restaurant when I froze.

There, right in front of me, were the Montreal Canadians. The same players we had watched on the ice the night before and the same players my Dad and I had watched so many times on TV during CBC's Hockey Night In Canada.

I quickly scanned the room and matched as many faces as I could to the names that I knew so well. Larry Robinson was there, and Ken Dryden. Pierre Mondou's at a table with Jacques Lemaire and Mario Tremblay's sitting at the table by the window.

This is unbelievable, I thought. *They are ALL here.* I noticed my Dad had stopped at a table and was shaking hands with someone. *Who is that?* I wondered. I couldn't see his face because my Dad was blocking my view so I took a few steps to my right to see for sure who it was.

"HoooooLeeeeeeeWaaaaaaaa," I said out loud when I could finally see who was at the table. My Dad had shaken hands with, and was now talking to, the great Guy Lafleur, my favorite player of all time. I walked slowly toward them, keeping my eyes fixed on Guy Lafleur. He was smiling and talking with my Dad in between sips of ice water. At that point I could really have used a sip of water myself. I was so nervous my mouth had gone bone dry. My legs were weak and the pen and paper in my hand felt like they weighed a ton. I walked up next to my Dad just as he turned to walk away.

"Oh there you are," he said to me as he turned back to face Lafleur.

"Mr. Lafleur, this is my son, Chris." My Dad took a step back to make room for me to take a step closer.

"Hello Chris. How are you?" he said in a heavy French Canadian accent as he extended his hand.

"Good," I answered, mustering only a faint whisper as I shook his hand and swallowed the huge lump in my throat.

"You are his favorite player. He's a little nervous right now," my Dad chimed in, knowing I had all I could do just to remain standing. Actually speaking at that point was just too much to ask of me.

"Could he get your autograph?" Dad asked as he nodded toward me and took the pen and paper from my hands.

"Sure," Lafleur said shooting a quick wink my way.

He signed his name, shook hands with my Dad again, and smiled as we walked away. Dad went through the same routine at a few other tables, introducing himself and then his extremely nervous son, helping me get more autographs and doing it all with the same excitement as a child on Christmas morning.

We watched the Twins and Tigers later that evening, but the game was kind of anti-climatic after our experience in the morning. It was always fun to go to the game and take in the sights and sounds of a major league baseball game, but I couldn't get breakfast out of my head. I didn't eat a thing, yet it was the greatest breakfast of my life. I have my Dad to thank for that.

You are never too old to have heroes and you can always be a kid at heart. Who knows, you might also become someone else's hero in the process?

Lesson #4: Take Responsibility For Your Actions

As a kid, every fall meant participating in the annual Punt, Pass, and Kick (P, P, &K) competition. Our local event was held on the football field at Michigan Technological University in Houghton. Age group winners of the local event would qualify for the district competition followed by zone competition and eventually the right to don full Green Bay Packers gear and compete during half time of a Packer game at legendary Lambeau Field. A dream come true.

In P, P, & K each participant punts, passes, and kicks a football for points based on distance and accuracy. The goal was to get the ball out as far as possible in each skill, but you also needed to keep it as close to the tape measure line as possible as accuracy points were deducted from your score the further the ball landed away from the line.

When I was 10, I won our local competition in Houghton as well as the district competition in Escanaba. Winning the latter event qualified me for the zone competition in Milwaukee and put me one step away from competing at Lambeau Field.

We arrived at the stadium in Milwaukee 30 minutes or so before the competition was to begin. It was very cold that morning, much colder than what I had competed in during the previous two competitions. Dad and I went to the registration table, completed the required paperwork, and found a spot on the field to practice. After 20 minutes or so my hands were so cold I could hardly grip the ball. My feet were frozen and felt like cement blocks on the end of my legs.   Every time I kicked or punted the ball it felt like I was using a brick. It was just hard to move in general, but we didn't have time to go to the car to warm up as the competition was set to begin.

Fifteen minutes into the competition my name was called and I stepped to the line. As per the event name, punting is the first of the three skills, followed by passing and kicking. I remember thinking, as I took the ball from the official, how glad I was it wasn't called Pass, Punt, & Kick because my hands were still so cold and throwing the ball at that point seemed next to impossible. I went through my pre-punt routine just like I had in every other competition. I turned the ball so the laces were facing up, letting it lie flat in the palm of my right hand, with the nose of the ball pointing slightly to the left. I took two steps, right foot then planting my left foot. I swung my right leg through and dropped the ball perfectly... only to miss it completely and watch it bounce on the ground beside me. I bent over, picked up the ball, and gave the front line official an awkward smile and nervous laugh as I stepped back up to the line to do it again. But now the line official stepped in front of me.

"Sorry son," he said. "That's it. You don't get a second chance to punt."

Immediately, I knew what that meant. There was no possible way I was going to win this competition with points from only two skills when everyone else was using three. My dream of competing at Lambeau was over and I was crushed. I didn't even want to complete the other two skills, but knew I had to finish.

Following the awards presentation, I finished tenth at best, I walked back to the car with Dad, carrying the football I had used in practice earlier that morning. As we got close to the car I stepped forward and punted the ball, watching it sail high over our car and far into the parking lot. I burst into tears wondering why I couldn't have done that when it counted.

On the drive home I made a point of complaining about pretty much everything. How the weather was so cold, which made me cold, which made it hard to do anything and how unfair it was that I didn't get a "do over" when I never even touched the ball with my foot on the attempted punt. Dad listened for a while and then he spoke.

"Listen," he said. "You can keep going on and on about all that stuff, but is that really to blame for you not winning? Everyone was out there in the same cold weather, blowing on their hands, and moving around trying to stay warm. Maybe you could have done some things differently that would have helped, but in the end you made a mistake and now it's over. Instead of blaming the weather and talking about how unfair the rules are, why don't you just take responsibility for how you handled it and consider it a learning experience. That's enough; I don't want to hear anymore."

Life is full of opportunities to make your dreams come true. Not everything is always going to go your way and it's much easier to blame others for your failures than it is to take responsibility for your own actions and the results that go with them.

Lesson #5: Preparation Creates Opportunity

We had just pulled into a parking spot at Milwaukee's County Stadium and my Dad was loading a new roll of film into his camera. As he clicked the film chamber shut he looked back over his right shoulder.

"Ready?" he asked me as he gathered his jacket.

"Yeah, let's go," I replied as I climbed out of the back-seat of our van.

"Don't forget your glove," he said. "You never know when one's going to come our way."

My Dad knew one of the main reasons why I loved to go to Brewers' games was for the chance to walk away from the park with a ball pitched, then hit, by a major league baseball player.

It wouldn't matter who it was or where it was. Just to have a souvenir like that was something I always wanted.

We made our way to the ticket office and my Dad asked if there were any box seats available.

"First base line or third base line?" asked the woman behind the counter.

"We'll take the third base line please," Dad replied as he reached for his wallet.

The woman pushed the tickets and a couple dollars worth of change back under the window toward my Dad. He picked them up, put the bills back into his wallet, and we headed for the entrance.

"Why did you pick the third base side, Dad?" I asked, pounding a fist into my glove.

"There are going to be a lot of lefties in the lineup tonight. Most of the foul balls hit by lefties go down the third base line. Righties hit them down the first base line," he
explained.

I had never heard that theory before, but now that we had tickets down the third base line and Dad said there were going to be a lot of lefties in the game, I was willing to buy it and found myself feeling a little extra excited about my chances to get a game ball.

We found our seats and I was surprised at how close we were to the field. We sat 10 or 12 rows behind the visitor's dugout, but it seemed like we were right on the field. I commented to my Dad about how green the outfield grass was, how perfect the infield dirt looked, and how the foul lines and batter's box were marked with perfectly straight lines.

"I wish I could play on a field like that. That's the nicest one I've ever seen," I said to my Dad while pointing my glove toward the field.

"That would be fun, wouldn't it?" he answered as he stood up from his seat. "If it makes you feel any better, this stadium has the best hot dogs in the majors and you CAN have one of those," he added. "What do you think?".

"Sure I'll have one," I answered while never taking my eyes off the perfectly manicured infield.

My Dad side stepped his way through our row and made his way up the steps to the concession stands. A few minutes later he returned with two hot dogs, two Cokes, and a box of popcorn.

"I need to find out if their popcorn is the best in the majors, too," he said raising his eyebrows and giving me a wry smile.

We ate our hot dogs and watched the grounds crew finish touching up the infield following batting practice. Soon after the starting lineups were announced, we stood for the National Anthem, and the game was finally underway. Each time a lefty would come to the plate I would slide toward the front of my seat to get in a better position to react should a foul ball come my way. Right handed hitters gave me a chance to relax a little, take another sip of my Coke, and try to determine if a foul ball hit down the first base line could somehow carom far enough and at crazy enough angles to somehow make it back over to the seats on the third base line.

Dad's theory was being proven over and over again. Righties sent foul balls into the crowd down the first base line and lefties into the crowd on the third base line. As the game went on I found myself glancing at the scoreboard every so often. Not to check the score, but instead, to see what inning the game was in and how much time I had left to try to get a ball. As the later innings passed I found myself getting more and more irritated as a righty came to the plate. With each lefty, I moved closer and closer to the edge of my seat and pounded my glove harder and faster as the sense of urgency increased as each inning ended.

Finally, in the bottom of the eighth inning, the opportunity I had been waiting for was right in front of me. A foul ball, off the bat of a left handed hitter, was directly above my head and coming straight down. I stood up, raising my glove hand above my head and using my free hand to balance against the crowd that was now closing in on me from all directions. The ball was coming down fast and it was spinning much faster than I had imagined it would. I wondered if I would be able to keep it from popping out of my glove. Just before the ball was to hit my glove a mass of hands went up in the air in front of it. We were all squished together, reaching high overhead, some with one hand and others with both. I heard a loud SMACK and knew someone got a hand on it even though I couldn't see it anymore as I was now banging around in the middle of the pack.

Suddenly, I saw the ball roll past my right foot and under the seat next to me. I reached down with my right hand, the hand without the glove, and grabbed the ball. I had just wrapped my fingers around it when a large tennis shoe came down hard on top of my hand. In a natural reaction I pulled my hand away quickly and the ball slipped from my grasp. For a split second it was free and I reached forward to pick it up again, but a hand came down out of the pile and just as quickly the ball was gone. I stood up, looked around to see who had the ball, and found the person sitting right next to me. The guy who tried to squash my hand, but instead squashed my dream, was now sitting next to me admiring the ball he would be taking home from County Stadium. He was laughing and joking about how crazy it was trying to get to it and he was showing it to everyone seated around us. He turned, looked at me with a smile, and offered the ball to me. Not to take home, just to look at. I wanted to tell him I had a pretty good look at it right before he stomped on my hand, but I just spun it around a few times and handed it back to him.

The game ended, we walked back to the car and I told my Dad exactly what happened when the foul ball came our way. I said, "I had it right in my hand until that guy stepped on it."

My Dad looked at me, smiled, and said, "You'll get another chance someday."

"I should have used my glove," I grumbled, pounding a fist into the glove one last time.

I didn't know when the next chance would come, but I did know one thing for sure. Before going to the ballpark I was going to check the lineups very closely. If there were a lot of lefties in the game, I was sitting in the box seats on the third base line.

Prepare ahead of time and you can put yourself in a better position for success. It won't guarantee things will go your way, but a little preparation can be the key to getting a good opportunity.

Lesson #6: Windows Of Opportunity Are Small, So Act Fast

Like football's Punt, Pass, and Kick competition baseball had its version called Pitch, Hit, and Run. You pitched for accuracy, hit for distance, and were timed running the bases.

When I was 13, I won our local competition in Houghton, MI and advanced to the district competition in Gladstone, MI. I had a baseball game scheduled for the same day as the district in Gladstone so Dad inquired with the district director on the possibility of me taking part in a competition elsewhere and competing only to acquire a score. As it turned out there was another district in Midland, MI the next weekend and they allowed me to compete and put my score in against the participants in Gladstone.

We made the drive to Midland and I took part in the competition, but we weren't sure how I would stack up against the others who had been in Gladstone a week earlier. It was just a few days later when I heard the phone ring while cleaning my bedroom. I heard footsteps coming toward my room and poked my head out to see who it was. Dad was approaching from his bedroom and he stopped when he saw me.

"Phone's for you," he said. "You can take it in here," he added pointing to his bedroom.

I answered the phone and it was a representative from Pitch, Hit, and Run calling to tell me I had scored high enough in Midland to take part in the next level of competition. It was being held at Metropolitan Stadium in Minneapolis, MN and included doing the hitting portion of the competition just prior to the start of the Minnesota Twins game with the Detroit Tigers. I was floored. I couldn't believe I was going to be on the field at Metropolitan Stadium and actually competing in front of fans at a Major League Baseball game. To top it all off I was going to see a game between my favorite team, the Twins, and Dad's favorite team, the Tigers. I thanked the gentleman for the good news and handed the phone to Dad so he could get all the details.

My Mom, Dad, and I flew to Minneapolis from Hancock the day before the competition. After checking in to our hotel we checked in for the banquet that evening and I was measured and sized for my uniform. My very own Minnesota Twins uniform to be worn during the competition. I was in heaven and couldn't wait to get on the field the next day.

On the day of the competition we were instructed to be at Metropolitan Stadium at 1 p.m. Once there we were given instructions on how the competition would be run and what the schedule would be for the rest of the day including that night's game between the Twins and Tigers. We were informed at that time the entire competition would be held that afternoon then the hitting portion would be repeated for the fans prior to the Twins' game. Your hitting score would count in the afternoon then done "just for show" in the evening.

Each age group had only two participants, but there were six age groups so there was a little dead time between your events as they put everyone in each group through the pitching portion before moving everyone to hitting, and then to running. We were told there might be some Twins' players coming out on the field to watch, sign autographs, and mingle so we were free to roam the field and sit in the dugout to kill time between events. I had just completed the pitching portion and took a seat in the Twin's dugout. My Mom and Dad were seated two or three rows behind the dugout taking it all in. I was watching the younger groups compete in the hitting event when I noticed someone sit down next to me on the dugout bench. I turned and saw Twins' pitcher John Verhoeven slide next to me.

"How's it going?" he asked. "Have you hit yet?"

"No I haven't. It's going to be a little while because this is the first group and I'm in the last. But so far it's going OK."

I glanced past Verhoeven and noticed Dad straddling the railing that separates the playing field from the first row of seats. He was climbing over, coming onto the field, with his camera in hand. I figured he had somehow gotten word of Verhoeven and I having a conversation and was coming in to capture the moment.

I was a little embarrassed though because he was the only Dad on the field and I was one of the two oldest players in the competition. My embarrassment quickly turned to curiosity as Dad looked at me in the dugout, but didn't stop walking. He just smiled and said, "Gene Mauch and Al Kaline" while pointing to center field. I looked to center field and there was, in fact, Gene Mauch the Minnesota Twins manager having a conversation with former Tiger great Al Kaline, who was working the Tigers' television broadcasts for WDIV. I remember thinking it was kind of odd that Gene Mauch was wearing boxer shorts with a long sleeved under-shirt, black knee-high socks, and black baseball shoes.

"Is that your Dad?" Verhoeven asked, nodding toward the man with the camera.

"Yeah, that's my Dad," I answered.

"Does he take a lot of pictures?" he asked.

"Yeah, he takes a ton of them," I said.

"Well, that will be a beauty," he said with a chuckle and nodding toward the two men standing in center field. "Mauch in his underwear."

Dad snapped a picture then turned to head back to his seat behind the dugout. He didn't stop to take a picture of me and Verhoeven, just smiled again on his way back, climbed over the railing and watched the rest of the competition.

We finished the hitting and running portions of the event and headed back into one of the rooms on the lower level of the stadium for something to eat.

"Dad, I couldn't believe it when I saw you climbing over the railing and coming onto the field," I said.

"Why is that?" he asked.

"Nobody else was out there taking pictures and then I see you coming down with your camera. I thought you were coming to take a picture of me sitting with John Verhoeven," I explained.

"Didn't you see who was out there?" he asked with wide eyes. "That was Al Kaline. He's going into the Hall of Fame! I heard the guy say you could roam the field and sit in the dugout so I when I saw him out there I decided to roam."

"I think he meant us, Dad," I said referring to the competitors.

"I didn't hear him say that. I just heard if you want to roam, go ahead," Dad explained matter of factly.

"Verhoeven said that picture will be a beauty because Gene Mauch's in his underwear," I said with a smile.

"I think it will be, too," Dad answered smiling back. "I can tell people I took the field with Al Kaline and have a picture to prove it. How many people can say that?"

Special moments in life come and go very fast. Be aware of what is going on around you and be able to act quickly. Doing so can turn those fleeting moments into memories that last forever.

Lesson #7: Be Generous

Back in high school, well before graphite shafts, composite sticks, one-piece "buy this stick and you'll shoot the puck like Bret Hull" super-stiff flex, weapons of mass goal scoring, I was always a Sherwood 5030 fan. Those hockey sticks were all wood, feather lite, and had just the right curve to the blade. Not the most durable stick, but I loved them. And you couldn't beat the price of $12 per stick. That brand was always a favorite of mine and many of my teammates at Hancock High School.

Stu and I had a pretty regular routine of accompanying each other to Weber's Sporting Goods in Houghton whenever one of us needed some new lumber.

I remember Stu coming to my locker after school one day and asking if I wanted to go to Weber's with him to get a new stick. I really needed one, but was trying to get the most out of the one I had since it seemed like I had already gone through a lot of them that season. Like a typical teenager I was low on cash….well, let's be honest, I was completely broke and would have to rely on Dad to buck up.

"I don't think I'm going to go, Stu," I told him.

"Why?" he asked.

"I'm out of cash," was my reply.

"Just ask B. Willy," Stu said referring to the nickname my friends gave my Dad.

"Naw. I don't want to do that. He just gave me some money yesterday and it's   already gone. I don't want to ask him for more."

I shut the door on my locker and turned to walk away.

"Gives," Stu said, so I stopped walking and turned back to face him. "Your Dad would give me 20 bucks if I asked him for it."

I kind of laughed as I knew that what Stu said was the truth. I didn't ask Dad for any money that day, but I did go to

Weber's with Stu and he bought a new Sherwood 5030 feather
lite.

**Be generous and helpful to others. The greatest com-
pliment you can get is that you've made someone feel like
you would do anything for them.**

Lesson #8 Be A Leader Not A Follower

One of the most intense rivalries in Michigan high school sports is found in the annual Copper Island Classic hockey series played between the Hancock Bulldogs and Calumet Copper Kings. Dating back to 1976 the "Classic" uses a two games, total goals format to determine the winner. Winning the series means taking home the prestigious John Sherf trophy which, during my playing career from 1981-1985, was presented to the winning teams' captains by Mr. John Sherf himself. Mr. Sherf grew up in Calumet and played hockey for the University of Michigan before playing professionally for the Detroit Red Wings.   He holds the distinction of being the first U.S. citizen to have his named engraved on the Stanley Cup as he helped the Red Wings win the cup during the National Hockey League playoffs in 1937. Mr. Sherf passed away in 1991, but I will always remember what an honor it was to be on the ice with him whether we won or lost.

I played in four 'Classics while in high school and can honestly say they were some of the greatest times in my life. Each year both games were played in the Calumet Armory on the Friday and Saturday following Thanksgiving.   I always loved playing in the Armory because the rink was very cold, the ice very fast, and the Calumet fans were rabid.

It wasn't uncommon for 2000 people to turn out for each of the games. The bleachers would be packed and fans would stand four or five deep around the glass. Whenever either of the teams would score it got so loud in the building you would swear the roof was going to fall. It was a tremendous atmosphere for a high school sporting event and one I wish every athlete could experience just once.

Each year the two teams were evenly matched.   As the overall series went Calumet held a 5-4 edge through the 1984 series which included them winning four straight from 1979-1982. Although we accepted the trophy from Mr. Sherf in both 1983 and 1984, the series I will remember most was played in 1982.

We went into Calumet for the '82 series determined to break the grip they had on the Sherf trophy as they had won it the past three years in a row. Friday night's game was the typical barn burner and went down to the wire.   Tied 3-3 late in the third period we scored with 3:12 left in the game and held on for a series opening 4-3 win.   We worked hard that night and felt good about going into Saturday's deciding game up by a goal and sitting in the driver's seat. We knew we didn't have to win on Saturday, due to the total goals format, we just couldn't get beat by two goals or more.   Easy enough. Or so we thought.

Exactly what happened on Saturday night, I'm still not sure.   For whatever reasons we looked like boys playing against men.   Calumet didn't take long to get on the scoreboard and quickly turned the game into a laugher. No matter what we did they had an answer. Our one goal lead going into Saturday's game ended up not meaning very much as we lost the second game 9-1 and the total goals series 12-5. Calumet had won the Sherf Trophy for the fourth year in a row and we were left with only a cold bus ride home.

Our drive from Calumet to our home ice at Houghton County Arena (HCA) in Hancock was only about 20 minutes long. Typically, our road trips all ended the same way. Our bus would pull up to the rink, we'd unload all of our gear, get in our cars and go home. Because I was a sophomore and not yet driving my Dad would usually meet me at the rink for a ride home. He liked to talk about the games on the short drive from HCA to our house. This night was the same as I noticed him waiting, in the family van, as soon as we pulled into the HCA parking lot.

Our bus had not yet come to a complete stop near the front door of the rink when our coach, Rick Miller, stood up from his first row seat and turned to face all of us in the back.

Before he spoke a word we could all tell, just by the look on his face, that he was not happy.

"OK boys," he snarled. "Get in there and put your gear back on. We're going to skate."

A collective groan moved through the bus, but Coach Miller wasn't having any of it.

"And if you're not on the ice in 15 minutes, don't bother showing up for practice on Monday because you're done," he added.

Are you kidding me? I thought. *It's almost midnight and we're going back on the ice?*

I pulled my gear off the bus and carried it, with my sticks, toward our van. I dropped everything on the ground next to the van and opened the front passenger side door.

"I can't leave yet Dad," I said. "Coach is making us go in and skate."

I was really mad, seeing red, and hoped Dad would say Coach's plan was ridiculous and there was no way he was going to allow it all to happen. Had he said, "Get in, we're leaving", I would have joined him and probably sacrificed the rest of my season in the process. Instead, I got the opposite.

"I'll be here when you're done," he said.

I stepped back, shook my head, and mumbled how I thought this whole thing was so stupid. Dad wasn't impressed.

"Did you guys expect Coach Miller to be happy about tonight's game?" he asked.

"Well no, but…" Dad didn't want to hear it so he didn't let me finish.

"You guys went up there tonight thinking you had it in the bag and you got it handed to you," he said. If I was him I would be mad, too," he added. "In fact, you should all be upset with yourselves because nobody was ready to play and you stunk the place up."

It was obvious no sympathy was coming my way so I stepped back from the door.

"I'll see you when we're done," I said and closed the door.

Everyone that was on the bus was also in the locker room and put their gear on. Nobody wanted to test Coach Miller's threat of being released from the team if you didn't participate in that evening's additional skate. I had wanted to, but Dad squashed that idea in a hurry.

We all dressed again, putting on cold, wet gear and making our way onto the ice surface at HCA. Our "skating party", as Coach Miller called it, started at 11:15pm and wrapped up at 12:30am. No shooting, no passing, no stick handling, no pucks period. It was strictly skating. We did every thigh burning skating drill Coach Miller could remember and finished the session with his favorite called the "Gut buster". After 75 minutes of sprints and periodic tongue lashings it was over and we were free to go home.

I showered, got dressed, and carried my gear outside. Dad was still there, just like he said he would be, so I loaded everything into the van and we left. Not much was said during the drive home, but at that point I was so dead tired I really didn't feel like talking anyway. All I wanted to do was get home and go to bed and I knew we would more than likely be talking about it again in the morning.

I slept late on Sunday, finally making my way downstairs around 10:30am. I went into the kitchen to pour a bowl of cereal and Dad was sitting at the counter looking through some old mail.

"How ya doing?" he asked.

"OK, I guess," I answered. "Sore and tired, but I should live."

Dad laughed and pushed the stack of mail into a pile in the center of the counter.

"Pretty disappointing last night, huh?" he asked.

"Yeah, the whole night was a disaster," I replied. "I'm sure Monday's practice won't be much fun, either."

"Well, there wasn't much leadership shown from any of you guys last night so maybe tomorrow would be a good time to start," he said. "You know a tough day's coming so some-one's got to take charge and do something with it," he added. "That's what you needed last night when Calumet had your backs against the wall. Someone to step forward and lead, to show you guys weren't going down without a fight. But it never happened."

"I just never thought we'd get beat that bad. There's no way they are eight goals better than us. No way," I said.

"On most nights, I would agree," he said. "But last night they were. They only needed to be three goals better to win the series, but they were leaving no doubt."

"Once they started pouring it on it just seemed like there was nothing we could do to stop the bleeding," I said.

"I thought you guys waited too long to start playing," he said. "When they went up by two goals, that's when someone needed to step forward and get you guys going. I was hoping maybe that would be you."

"I'm a sophomore, Dad." I said.

"So what?" he replied.

"So....the juniors and seniors don't want someone younger telling them what to do," I explained.

"I'm not saying you should have started barking out instructions to everyone," he said. "In fact, you wouldn't have needed to say anything. A lot of guys can talk a good game, but often times that talk is cheap."

"What was I supposed to do then?" I asked.

"Just lead by example," he said. "Work hard, put a few really good shifts together and hope it gets contagious. That's where maybe your age would work for you when you think it's working against you."

"How's that?" I asked.

"Maybe the older guys start thinking they don't want to get shown up by a sophomore," he said. "If that's what lights a fire under them, so be it."

At that point I started to realize how I had been kind of tip toeing around so to speak, in the locker room, during practice, and during the games. I was always careful of what I said and never wanted anyone to think I was over stepping my bounds as an underclassmen. I had never really thought about how my actions could be so much more powerful than what I said. Until that time I felt only the team captains could be considered the team leaders. A captain's "C" on the front of their jersey, almost exclusively reserved for seniors, meant they were the people to speak up, give the pre-game rah rah speeches, and lead our team on the ice. Whether or not they actually went out and did what they said they were going to do was never really given a second thought.

"Whether it's hockey or anything else you'll always be happier if you're a leader versus a follower," Dad said.

"Why is that?" I asked.

"Because," he answered. "Leaders make things happen. They see something out there they want and they find a way to go get it. Followers see them being successful, time after time, and the natural reaction is for them to want to join in and have that same success," he explained.

"So the follower's end up being successful, too?" I asked with a hint of confusion.

"It can work out that way, but the big difference is followers are leaving their success to chance and to decisions made by someone else. It's much easier to accept the outcome of any situation, good or bad, when you take the lead and make decisions on your own based on what you think is best," he said. "The bottom line is, leaders have a good idea of where they want to go and how to get there. Followers are OK when things go their way, but when they don't, all you hear from them is complaining about where they are, how they got there, and whose fault it is. Of course, it's never any fault of their own."

I started to give some serious thought to how the previous night's game played out and how I now wished I had handled things differently. Maybe it would not have made a difference in the final score, but I knew I would have felt better if I could honestly say I gave it my all the entire game. Instead I knew, once things started to go bad and Calumet was pulling away, I had given in to all the grumbling, finger pointing, and complaining. I had done the same because I had been a follower instead of a leader. We still had a full season ahead of us and I made a vow that Sunday morning to really work at being more of a leader. It wasn't in my nature to do a lot of talking so I took Dad's advice and focused on leading with my play.

As it turned out we won the regional championship that year and didn't have to participate in any additional late night skating parties. We were one win away from playing in Hancock's first ever state semifinal game, but lost to Sault Ste. Marie in the quarter final game 3-2 and our season was over. I always hated to lose, but even though we had just lost our biggest game of the year, I had a feeling of content. I felt that I could look myself in the mirror and honestly feel good about how I had handled things that night in terms of my play, my attitude, and my leadership.

Unless you are running for President, leadership has no age requirement. Whether or not you are a good leader doesn't necessarily depend on what you say it's often determined by what you do.

Lesson #9: Differentiate Yourself

Following my sophomore year in high school I started to receive some attention from different colleges and universities. Most of this attention was from football programs with a few hockey contacts sprinkled in as well.

I say it was "some" attention because college coaches and/or recruiters can't legally speak or meet with a high school sophomore. It was just the standard form letters saying that I had been referred to such and such as a potential student athlete, please fill out this questionnaire and return it so we have your information on file. Not really anything to brag about, but it was pretty neat to receive those official looking letters in the mail.

Every so often a new letter would arrive and Dad would read it and tell me what he knew about that particular school and team, like who the coach was, where they were located, the conference they were in, etc. If he didn't know, he was digging out an old Sports Illustrated, The Sporting News, whatever he could get his hands on that might have some specific school information we could discuss.

After bringing in the mail one day, I was sitting at the kitchen table, drinking a soda and flipping through the day's delivery of junk mail, bills, and catalogs. I could hear Dad coming down the steps and knew he would be looking for the mail.

"Any letters today?" he asked.

"Nope. None today." I replied.

Dad quickly looked through the stack of mail and didn't find much of interest. "Just bills, huh? Just bills."

He pulled a chair away from the table and sat down. Gently, he took off his glasses, rubbed his eyes, and put the glasses back on.

"I've been meaning to talk to you about something," he said.

Oh boy, I thought. *Here it comes. The birds and the bees talk that we've never had and one I just assumed we were*

*never going to have if it hadn't happened by sixth grade or so.
I am too old for this now....really.*

Everyone has that sense about some conversations being uncomfortable just before they start. In this case my senses were on high alert.

"You're starting to get some attention from these colleges," Dad said. "It's quite possible at some point down the road one of these schools could offer you a scholarship to come and play for them."

"Yeah, that would be pretty cool," I replied nervously, still not sure the birds and bees had flown away.

"In order to give yourself the best chance of that happening, you really need to make sure you take care of your grades," Dad said. "No matter how good you are there is always going to be someone out there who is just as good or better. Someone who is just as big, just as fast, and just as strong."

Dad took off his glasses again and rubbed his eyes, the sure sign that he was passionate about what he was saying.

"The thing you need to do is differentiate yourself from all those other guys. One way you can do that is by keeping good grades. There are plenty of good athletes out there, but not all of them do well in the classroom," he said.

"Any good coach is going to pay attention to that because they aren't going to want to give scholarship money to someone who isn't going be able to play because they fail their classes. You've got a couple of years to really focus on your grades, and separate yourself, to make sure you're in a smaller pool of players these schools are watching."

It made perfect sense to me and it had been a dream of mine to play college football or hockey since I was very young. By this time I had also developed a dream of getting a scholarship so I could remove the burden of paying for college from my parents. I already had an older sister attending Michigan Tech and three younger brothers coming up behind me. How my parents were going to pay for all of us to attend college, I didn't know. But I thought that if I could at least take care of my own situation through an athletic scholarship, that would take some financial pressure off my parents.

Through my junior year and into my senior year I focused on my homework and having good study habits. Dad would make sure to ask every so often how my classes were going and he was always interested in getting an early look at my report cards. In January of my senior year I was invited to visit Central Michigan University to tour the campus and meet with head football coach, Mr. Herb Deromedi. I visited the school the day after Super Bowl Sunday with both of my parents.

We met with the University's President and had a brief meeting with Coach Deromedi. Coach D, as he was known, explained that they were interested in having me become a member of the football team at CMU and that they were pre-pared to offer me a partial scholarship. Their plan was to bring in two punters, me being one of them, offering both half scholarships and letting the two of us fight it out for playing time. Coach D said he'd give me a couple of days to think about their offer and he would have one of his Assistant Coaches, Mr. Tom Kearly, follow up with me on Tuesday of the next week.

On the drive back to Hancock, most of the car talk was about CMU and our meeting with Coach D. All three of us agreed it was a nice campus, the football facilities were solid, and the partial scholarship was a good offer. I personally liked the fact that both the city of Mount Pleasant and the CMU campus were not overwhelmingly huge. It seemed pretty easy to navigate around the various lecture halls on campus, and the dorms were bigger and nicer than what I expected. Having the chance to play Division I college foot-ball, again the opportunity to have a dream come true, and get part of my education paid for was definitely moving my deci-sion toward CMU.

The following Tuesday morning, back in school, an office aide poked her head into my third hour study hall and called my name.

"Chris Givens?" she asked.

I raised my hand. "Here," I said slowly standing up from behind the desk.

"Someone's here to see you. Please go to the Athletic Director's office."

I wondered who it was and had a suspicion it might be Coach Kearly. As I entered the office from the main hallway I could see my Dad standing outside of an internal office, laughing and talking with someone. As I got closer I realized it was, in fact, Coach Kearly.

My Dad turned to face me, smiling bigger than I had seen in quite a while, and   stepped back so I could see who was there.   Coach Kearly stepped toward me, extending his hand, and asked how I was doing. We shook hands and he explained he had come to follow up on Coach D's offer. He also mentioned they had made a change and decided they weren't going to bring in two punters after all. They had decided to offer me a full scholarship instead and Coach Kearly wanted to know if that was going to be a good enough offer for us to move forward.

I was floored. In all honesty, I was pretty happy to have been offered a partial scholarship. To now have a "full ride" in front of me was unreal. Dad was obviously excited and he shook my hand firmly. "Congratulations." he said.

"Yes, this is great. I really appreciate it and I'm looking forward to joining the Chippewa football program," I said sheepishly as I shook Coach Kearly's hand again.

"Excuse me, Tom," my Dad said. "I just have to ask you a question. Why the new offer?"

Coach Kearly responded. "Well, we were also going to bring in this other boy from Fenton, but his grades are not very strong and Herb is concerned about whether or not he'll be around long term if his grades at CMU don't hold up. We don't feel Chris is a grade risk, so we decided to give him the full scholarship and not offer anything to the other player."

As it turned out, the boy from Fenton accepted a scholarship to play football at Western Michigan University. He also did not attend WMU for long. He left after the first semester due to poor grades.

Find ways to differentiate yourself from others. No matter what you are doing, there is always going to be someone who can do it just as good or better than you. Focus your efforts where others can't, or won't, and you'll end up ahead.

Lesson #10: Focus on what you can control; Don't worry about what you can't.

Going into my freshman year at CMU I didn't expect to be the starting punter, but thought I could probably get at least a little bit of playing time. Our starter was a fifth year senior who had the job the previous season, so I knew I would have to really out kick him in practice to have any prayer of playing in the games. Being as good wouldn't be good enough. As it turned out I didn't see any game time my freshman year, but there were plenty of lessons to be learned. One, in particular, more valuable than the others.

It was a Thursday afternoon and we had just taken the field at Kelly Shorts Stadium for practice. We were preparing to play Eastern Michigan at home that week and were anxious to get lined up against an interstate rival. As I sat stretching with the other punters and kickers, Coach D came up behind me and slapped a hand on my right shoulder pad.

"Are you ready to go this week?" he asked with a big smile on his face.

At first I couldn't tell if his smile meant he was joking or if he was just excited to be giving me news I had been waiting for all season.

"Yeah, I'm ready to go Coach," I answered, still trying to determine his sincerity.

"Well good 'cause you're getting some playing time this week. We want to put you in a game situation and see what you can do."

And with that coach turned and walked away.

I looked at the others around me and must have had a stunned look on my face.

"You gonna be all right, Gives?" asked Brian Tierney, a fellow kicker out of Grand Rapids.

"Do you think he's serious?" I asked to nobody in particular.

"Oh yeah, he's serious," Tierney replied. "Gives is in the game, baby!"

I couldn't wait for practice to be over so I could go back to the dorms and call my Dad with the good news. Once Coach D blew the final whistle to signal practice was over, I was in and out of the locker room in record time. I was starving, but there was no way this phone call could wait until after dinner. I pulled into a parking spot at Thorpe Hall, sprinted for the door, and climbed the stairs three at a time. By the time I got to my room I was shaking so badly I could hardly get my key in the door. It felt like it took me forever. I opened the door and immediately grabbed the phone and started to dial. I could feel my heart pounding and thought it might actually pop through my shirt. My Dad answered the phone.

"Hey Dad," I said.

"Chris, what are you up to? You sound out of breath," he answered.

"I just got back from practice," I said.

"Wow, must have been some practice if you're still breathing that hard," he joked.

"No, it's not that. I just ran up to my room from the parking lot because I wanted to call you right away," I said.

"Oh yeah? Why is that?" he asked.

"I'm playing on Saturday," I told him as a bead of sweat made its way down my nose.

"You are? That's great!" he yelled. The phone became muffled on his end, as he put the phone to his shirt, but I could still hear him. "Hey Mom, Chris is playing on Saturday!". His voice became clear again. "We're really happy for you."

"Coach just came out of the locker room at the beginning of practice and told me he was putting me in the game Saturday against Eastern," I explained. I had stopped shaking and my breathing was now under control. The sweat continued.

"Wow, that's exciting news. Congratulations. Your brother has a game in L'Anse Friday night, but we'll just leave right from there and drive straight through," he said.

"You could just leave early in the morning and still get here in time. You don't have to drive all through the night," I told him.

"Yeah, we could, but that doesn't leave any extra time. If we need to change a flat tire or something else goes wrong we might miss it," he explained. "I'll feel better if we just drive through the night. We'll have a chance to sleep for a few hours once we get down there."

We finished the conversation and I was finally able to make it to the cafeteria for dinner. I ate, then tried to do some homework, but my thoughts kept taking me to Saturday and my first playing time in a Division I college football game. I had dreams about it many times as a kid, but now the time had come and it was real. Saturday couldn't come fast enough.

On Saturday morning I was up early. Too nervous to sleep, I ate breakfast in the cafeteria then drove to 7-11 for a Big Gulp and copy of the Detroit Free Press. At 10 a.m. and unable to stand it any longer, I put on my "game day" dress and headed to the locker room. Just before leaving the dorm our phone rang. I answered it with one foot out into the hallway. It was my Dad.

"Hey Chris," he said. "Just wanted to let you know we made it. The ride down was fine and it went pretty fast with next to no traffic on the road."

"That's good. I was just about out the door," I said and stepped back into my room.

"Oh yeah? Where are you headed?" he asked.

"To the stadium," I answered.

"Already? I thought the game didn't start until one o'clock?" he asked sounding confused.

"It does, but I'm really nervous and just need to get down there and get the routine going," I explained.

"Nervous, huh?" he said. "Today's a big day. I guess I would probably be a little nervous too. Well, I'll let you get going then. Good luck."

"Thanks Dad. I'll see you guys after the game." I hung up the phone and headed for Kelly Shorts Stadium.

I wasn't sure what Coach D's plan was for getting me in the game. I didn't know if it would be in the first quarter or if he'd wait to see how things were going and then put me in later in the second half. He didn't say and I didn't ask so I took the same approach I did every game. Be ready at the start of each offensive possession and you'll know by third down whether or not you're getting the call.

With the start of each possession I could feel my heart start to race. This game was different because I knew at some point I would be going in. The first quarter ended and Coach D had not called my name. Same thing in the second quarter, but now I grew more anxious because I knew it was going to happen sometime in the next 30 minutes of play. We came out after half time and I took a little extra time to stretch and get loose before the third quarter began. As the third quarter ended, Coach D had still not called my name. As the final minutes of the fourth quarter ran off the clock I knew that it was not, in fact, going to happen. My first game experience would have to wait for another day. I was mad and didn't understand why Coach would tell me he was putting me in, get my all hyped up, and then not do it. What was worse for me though, was the fact that my parents drove eight hours through the early morning because I told them I was going to be playing. I showered, got dressed, and left the locker room to meet up with my parents. They were standing in the end zone underneath the goal posts waiting for me. I walked up to them and found it hard to look them in the eye.

"I'm really sorry," I said.

"Sorry for what?" Dad asked.

"That you guys drove all through the night thinking I was going to play and then I don't see a second of playing time," I said, staring straight down at the artificial turf.

"Oh that's OK", Dad said. "At least we got to see a good game."

We beat Eastern 17-10.

"I don't know why he does stuff like that?" I said referring to Coach D. "Why tell me I'm going to play and then not
follow through? I don't get it."

"Well, he's making decisions based on what he feels will
give your team the best chance to win," my Dad explained.
"That's his job. He's paid to make those decisions and his
livelihood depends on him making good ones. Today, those
decisions didn't include you. Maybe next Saturday will be
different."

"I don't know. I just wish he would have followed
through," I said now able to raise my head and look at my
Dad.

"Look," he said. "All you can do is go out and practice
as hard as possible. Kick the snot out of the ball and try to
make it impossible for him to keep you out of the game.
That's all you can do. Whether or not he decides to put you
in isn't something you can control so there's no point in you
worrying about it."

We played four more games that year and I didn't see
playing time in any of them. I did, however, establish a new
theme for my off season training. I was going to work out all
summer with one thing in mind. That is, making it next to
impossible for Coach D to keep me out of the game.

**Stay focused on the things you can control. Worry-
ing and stressing about things you can't control is a waste
of both time and energy.**

Lesson #11: Don't take yourself too seriously

I was fortunate enough to be named the starting punter for CMU's football team in the fall of 1986, my sophomore year. On the Sunday following each game, Coach D and his staff would select "Players Of The Week" for the offense, defense, and specialty teams. During the Sunday evening team meeting, the winners were announced and those players were invited to attend the weekly Chippewa Club luncheon at the Embers restaurant. The Chippewa Club is similar to a sports booster club and one of the perks offered to members is a seat at the weekly luncheon with the football coaching staff and individual Players Of The Week.

After a tough loss on the road to Kent State I was named the Specialty Teams' Player of the Week. It wasn't because of my punting, but more because of my ability to catch errant snaps from center. For whatever reasons, on that particular day, our long snapper was sending the ball everywhere except directly to me. His snap would sail way high, then way to the right, way to the left, then he'd bounce one to me. Keep in mind, punting in the college game is very different from punting in high school. You've got a second or two to get it away, with a perfect snap, so when things go wrong from center it only complicates things. I managed to handle each snap, get the punt away, and had nothing blocked.

As far as my average, it was not the most stellar punting performance, but it got the attention of the coaching staff and I was given that week's award. I looked forward to my first Chippewa Club luncheon and being one of the honored guests. Prior to food being served Coach D introduced each player at the head table and said a few words about their performance in that week's game. When everyone had finished eating he opened the floor for questions. A woman in the crowd raised her hand and Coach D pointed to her for the next question.

"Given Chris' performance on Saturday it looks as though he's got pretty good hands," she said. "Have you ever thought about using him as a receiver?"

Coach D smiled and, fighting through a chuckle, replied "Well, let's just say Chris has some serious speed limitations."

Coach D laughed, the Chippewa Club laughed, and my teammates laughed. I, on the other hand, couldn't find a way out quick enough.

"OK, great, very funny," I thought. "Just get on with the next question."

Coach answered questions for another 10 or 15 minutes then dismissed the players for practice. I drove back to the stadium for practice with my "tail between my legs" and couldn't stop thinking about how embarrassing lunch was. I had really looked forward to being at the head table and feeling proud of earning my seat there. Instead, I left focusing on one comment that had me wrecked for the day.

After practice, I ate dinner in the Thorpe Hall cafeteria and headed back to my dorm room. My Dad had asked that I call him after the luncheon to let him know how it went. I was still fuming when I made the call home. As was just about always the case, my Dad answered the phone. "Hey Dad," I said.

"Heeeeyyyyyy, it's Chris," he replied. "How was the luncheon today?"

I went on to tell him how I was the topic of an early question and what Coach's answer was. As soon as I got the word "limitations" out, my Dad started to laugh and he laughed loud and hard. It seemed like he laughed for 10 minutes, but it was probably only a few seconds. After gathering himself, he was again able to speak.

"Really?" he asked. "That's too funny. What a great answer."

"What a great answer? Dad, that was in front of the whole Chippewa Club!". I couldn't believe he wasn't as upset as I had been.

"Oh c'mon. Don't take yourself so seriously. What did you tell me your 40 yard dash time was, 4.9 or something like that?" he asked.

"Yeah, that's what it was," I said still looking for some support.

"Well then, that makes you too slow to be a receiver and you're not big enough to be a lineman so I guess you're in the right spot," he said. "Punters don't have to be fast and they don't have to be big. They just have to have a strong leg and good hands. You've got both."

"But Dad, Coach embarrassed me in front of everyone, don't you understand?" I pleaded with him almost begging for him to say something about how Coach was out of line.

"Listen, you've got to lighten up. So he came back with something and got a good laugh out of it. It would have been really funny if you would have thought of it and gave that same answer to the crowd yourself. A little self deprecating humor can go a long ways."

"Self deprecating humor?" I asked. "I don't even know what that means."

"You need to be confident enough to make fun of yourself sometimes. Look at it this way, I tell people all the time that I'm not fat, I'm just really short for my weight."

I laughed, he laughed, and by the time I hung up the phone it was all good. I made a vow that I was going to really make an effort to not be so sensitive anymore. As time went on my Dad was often asked to be the Master of Ceremonies at various dinners and fundraisers back in Hancock. After each one people commented on how funny he was and how they looked forward to seeing him "perform" the next time. Of course, the reason people thought he was so funny was because he used self deprecating humor perfectly.

Be confident and comfortable with who you are. We are all going to look silly sometimes and it is OK for people to notice.

Lesson #12: Give Respect, Earn Respect

As mentioned earlier, Little League baseball was a very big part of my life as a child. I started playing when I was eight-years-old and my three younger brothers played as well. My Dad, although never an athlete himself, coached Little League teams for many years in Hancock. He coached my teams, those of all my brothers, and continued to coach well after my youngest brother, Tim, had played his final year in the program. Dad was also asked to coach many of the local all star teams, an honor he took great pride in.

If you look strictly at wins and losses you would, without a doubt, consider Dad a very successful coach. I can't tell you what his overall record was because we never talked about won and loss records and he never seemed to keep count. I do know, however, his teams were always very successful and won numerous league championships. But where he really created his coaching legacy is in how he treated his players and the tremendous amount of respect they, and their parents, had for him and how that same level of respect continues today. This, in my opinion, made him a great coach regardless of how many games his teams won or lost.

In 1995, I was named the head hockey coach at Traverse City Central High School. I had been an assistant to Jude Cummings for the three seasons prior and Jude had decided to retire from coaching after the 1994-95 season.   I was extremely excited to take on this position and relished the thought of now being able to call all of the shots. At the same time I had absolutely no head coaching experience and in the back of my mind I wondered if I was really ready to take on the job. An assistant coach's duties are very different from those of the head coach, and I knew that very well. But I also knew I had a great source I could go to for help and guidance in my new position.

I called Dad to let him know I had been officially named the head coach. He was excited and mentioned several times how "that job comes with a lot of responsibility." I agreed with him and was honest about my feelings.

"I'm really excited, Dad, but I'm kind of feeling like maybe I'm getting in over my head," I said.

"Why's that?" he asked.

"Well, I guess it's just that I've watched Jude over the past three years and know how much work goes into being the head coach. I've never been in this position before and I'm feeling kind of overwhelmed."

"Oh, you'll be fine," Dad assured me, but he always did that when I had self doubt whether he truly believed it or not.

"Any advice for me on this?" I asked.

"I could give you lots of advice, but that would take forever," he said. "A lot of it you'll just have to deal with as you're going along. I think if you use two or three key things as your foundation, and build on it from there, you will do really well."

"So what are those?" I asked.

"Well first," he said, "You have to earn your respect. There's a certain level of respect that comes with being a coach, but to really get your kids to buy in to what you want them to do they have to truly respect you not only as a coach, but as a person also. In order for that to happen you have to treat your players with a very high level of respect. Never embarrass a player in front of his teammates. That is one of the worst things you could do."

"Secondly," he added, "Your players need to know that you care about them as people and not just as hockey players. If they know you care about them and what's going on in their lives you will develop some strong relationships that will be key when your team gets into a tough situation. Take time to talk to your players about other things going on in their lives. Talk about school, their families, girlfriends, grandparents, all the other things that are important to them.

"And the last thing, Chris. Use all of your players. Don't make anyone sit on the bench for the whole game,

game after game. There's just no reason for it and it's the fastest way to killing the team's chemistry. One guy gets mad and tries to get everyone around him to jump on his band-wagon and if you've got two or three guys that aren't happy it can snow ball into a huge mess. There are always opportunities to use different guys and you've got to make sure everyone plays. They don't need to play equally, obviously, but give everyone an opportunity. Nobody needs to sit on the bench the whole game every game."

"That's easier said than done, Dad," I answered.

"Why do you say that?" he asked.

"It just is," I answered.

"If you don't feel someone is good enough to play in the games then you shouldn't take them in the first place," he said. "Besides, what are you really playing for?"

"What do you mean?" I answered.

"You would like to win the conference championship, right?" he asked.

"Yeah," I answered.

"And you've got a tournament or two in there you'd like to win also, right?" he added.

"Right," I replied.

"Hopefully you guys jell at the right time, get hot in the playoffs, and make a run toward a state championship, right?" he said.

"Yeah, that would be awesome," I answered.

"You've got a number of non-conference games mixed in there, too?" he asked

"Yeah, not many, but there's a few," I told him.

"So early in the season you play a non-conference game and you play everyone the whole game. The other team shortens their bench, their big guns play some shifts against your fourth liners, and this means you lose the game. What's the big deal?" he asked.

"It's not a big deal, I guess." I answered, but not truly sure I believed it myself. My Dad could sense my hesitation and he continued.

"Look, you can shorten your bench too, but do it in the big games. Why shorten your bench in games that have no bearing on your team's other goals when you can use those opportunities to help kids develop? You may not have a deep team to begin with, but you can be a deep team by the end of the season. What if you run into a situation when one of your big guns gets hurt or sick and can't play. What do you do then? You will need guys to step in and take their place. If they've never been given the chance before they aren't going to be able to do their best. What if that happens in a playoff game? Do you want to have to call on someone who's never been given much of an opportunity before? That can't be the first time they've done it."

He drilled away with point after point that made it hard to argue.

"I hadn't really thought of it that way to be honest with you," I confessed.

"Giving everyone a chance to play shows you have confidence in them," he said. "If you show confidence in them, it helps build their desire to play and with that you'll notice they play harder and harder with each shift. When everyone plays they all feel part of the team and it helps build chemistry. When you keep someone on the bench for the whole game every game it's embarrassing for the player and, again, embarrassing your players in front of their teammates is bad. Use them all, treat them well, and let them know you care about them as people and not just hockey players. They will respect you for respecting them and you'll be on your way."

The coaching advice my Dad gave me that day has served the hockey program well at Traverse City Central. Never was it more key than in 2006 when we won the Division 2 State Championship at Compuware Arena in Plymouth,

MI. We played that game, and the majority of our schedule, with three freshmen who saw a regular shift and played pivotal roles on our special teams.

In the state final we were nursing a 2-1 lead over Saline late in the third period. We took a penalty and two of our four players on the ice were freshmen. We killed the penalty, rode out the rest of the time on the clock and won the first state championship in Traverse City high school hockey history. The players who were called upon answered the call and performed. Then again, they had done it all before... just like Dad had told me they would.

Whether you are in charge of a sports team or a group of employees, the level of respect you earn depends on the level of respect you give. How you treat people can be a significant factor in how they perform.

Lesson #13: Be Strong And Keep A Sense of Humor Even In The Face Of Adversity

My Dad was first diagnosed with diabetes in 1975 when I was 8-years-old. I remember visiting him in the hospital and watching him practice insulin shots on an orange. Of course, I didn't know exactly what diabetes was at that time and both of my parents downplayed it so I wouldn't worry too much. I was told Dad would be in the hospital for a few days, but everything was going to be fine. As time went on, everything did go reasonably well for Dad in living with this disease.

Each morning, before eating breakfast, he would give himself an insulin shot and then get on with his day. Not a big deal. I never knew the diabetes to really keep him from doing any of the things he enjoyed. It would be the cause of an interruption sometimes, but it never stopped him completely. For example, if I noticed him start to sweat really bad, for no obvious reason, it was typically a sign that he was starting feel the effects of low blood sugar.

"Are you okay, Dad?" I would ask.

"Yeah, I'm all right. Just feeling a little woozy," was his standard answer. When he used the term "woozy," I knew it meant he needed to eat something to help get his blood sugar back in line. If we were away from home he did a pretty good job of making sure some hard candy, fruit, or anything else that was quick and easy for him to get to was in the car. We'd take a break from whatever we were doing, he'd eat, have something to drink, and was fine. If only that was all there was to it.

As is the case with almost all diseases diabetes has the power to pack a huge punch full of ugly complications. Over the years it seemed like every time my Dad came home from a doctor's appointment, a new ailment was being treated and they were all tied to diabetes. With each new diagnosis came a new prescription and at one time it seemed like he had a stack of 25 different pills to take every morning. It became clear that what initially started as a very manageable condition had grown into something very, very serious.

Once I left Hancock for CMU, my Dad and I always talked on the phone at least once per week. That continued when I moved to Traverse City and the phone calls were often more frequent during the winter once the high school hockey season started. Dad would want to know how practices were going, how the team was coming together, and what I thought we needed to do to beat that week's opponent. My Dad would often call on Sunday mornings to get details on that weekend's series even though it would have been cheaper for him to just wait for his Traverse City Record Eagle newspaper subscription to deliver all of those details a day or two later. In December 1998 I received a call from home, but it wasn't my Dad. It was my brother, Greg.

"Hey," he said.

"What's up?" I asked.

"Well, Dad got really sick about an hour ago and had to be taken to the hospital. He was throwing up blood really bad and it doesn't sound good," he said. "They've been giving him blood since he got to the hospital, but he just keeps throwing up and can't keep it in him."

"Why?" I asked. "Any idea what's happening?"

"No, but I haven't really been able to talk to anyone except Mom. She's up there with him, but it was a pretty short conversation."

Then he added. "Chris, I don't know if he's going to make it."

It felt like someone pulled back and drove a sledgehammer into my stomach. I couldn't breath, I couldn't think straight, but I didn't want to fall apart in front of my wife and son. I took a few long, deep breaths, and tried to get myself together.

"Okay," I answered, my voice quivering. "Let me know if you hear anything else. I'm going to try to call Mom."

When you receive a phone call like that your first thought is you want to be there, with your family, right that second. You want to know exactly what is going on, how serious the situation really is, and what is being done to fix it. I had very little information to go on other than my Dad was very, very sick, losing blood quickly, and might not make it. Your mind races and the waiting and wondering are excruciatingly painful. On top of that, I was 386 miles away in Traverse City, but it may as well have been a million miles. For the first time in a very long time I was scared, feeling very helpless and alone. I hung up the phone and headed straight for the bedroom knowing the tears were coming no matter how hard I tried to hold them back. I didn't want my son, Cam, to see his own Dad cry.

My wife, Jen, had heard most of the conversation from the living room and was now following me down the hallway.

"It's your Dad, isn't it?" she asked.

"Yeah," I said, blinking back tears. "Greg said he doesn't know if he's going to make it."

And with that, I lost it. I hadn't cried like that since I was a little boy.

"Oh honey," she said rubbing her hand on my back. "I'm so sorry. Let's try to stay positive and we'll pray for him to pull through this."

Several hours passed and there were no updates. I couldn't take it anymore.

"I have to talk to someone up there," I said to Jen.

I dialed directory assistance and got the number for the hospital in Hancock. I called, asked to be connected to Bill Givens' room, and got through right away. My Mom answered the phone.

"Hello?" she said.

"Hi Mom," I answered.

"Oh Hi," she said sounding surprised.

"How is Dad doing?" I asked.

"He seems to be doing OK right now. He's sleeping and the doctor said he will probably be pretty tired for a while. He's been through a pretty big ordeal," she explained, her voice very calm and reassuring.

"What happened?" I asked.

"We're not sure," she said. "He starting bleeding internally for some reason and the blood just kept coming out. He was throwing up like crazy."

"Geez," I said, not able to come up with anything more.

"Should I come home?" I asked.

"No, I don't think you need to," Mom said. "They seem to have everything under control now and he's resting. Let's wait and see what tomorrow brings and we can decide then."

I didn't sleep well that night at all. The 'stay vs. go' battle was raging in my head and I couldn't stop thinking about my Mom's description of the incident. It seemed like it took forever for morning to come. Shortly after 8 a.m., I called my Mom again.

"How is he doing today?" I asked.

"Oh, OK I guess," Mom answered. "He was awake for a little while early this morning, but he's sleeping again now," she added.

"So what are they telling you?" I asked, assuming their had to be some new information about what caused Dad to get so sick.

"Nothing new really," she replied.

"And he's going to make it now, right?" I asked trying to sound sure, but the uneasiness in my voice was impossible to miss.

"Well, his doctor said he's not out of the woods yet," she said.

"So I should probably come home then?" I asked.

"He's not out of the woods, but he's certainly much better than when we got here yesterday. I don't think you should come home. I will let you know if things change," she said.

"OK," I answered, knowing the restless night I had gone through the night before was sure to repeat itself over and over again until I knew for sure Dad was going to be okay. A few days passed and with each phone call I learned Dad was making small, steady improvements each day. He had tubes down his throat that prevented him from speaking, but everything else seemed to be coming around well.

When the tubes were finally removed he was able to speak, but his throat was sore and conversations were kept short. I hadn't talked to him since he was taken to the hospital so I was anxious to finally get the chance. His voice was rough and I had to listen hard to understand him, but it was great to hear his voice.

"Hi Dad," I said.

"Hi. How are you doing?" he asked.

"I'm good. The more important question is how are YOU doing?" I asked.

"I'm OK....now," he said. "My doctor told me I was flirting with the angels there for awhile," he said with a laugh although I didn't find it very funny. "He said they were dancing all around me and I almost joined them." he added.

"That sounds bad," I said. "I asked Mom if I should come home, but she told me to stay in Traverse City. I still feel like I should be up there with you."

"No, no, no," Dad said adamantly. "You don't need to come here. I'm going to be fine and there's nothing for you to do here anyway."

"I know, but I just feel like I should be there." I said.

"You don't need to worry about your Dad." he said. "I'm fine. You have your family to take care of down there. And, you have to stay with your hockey team. Those kids need you," he added. "Don't you have a big tournament coming up?" he asked.

"Everything is OK," he said. "You need to be where you're needed the most and that is right where you are now."

I felt much better after finally talking to my Dad. It was good to hear his voice, as gravelly as it was, and have him tell me himself that he was OK. Even though, at that particular moment, hockey didn't seem very important to me, I had to smile when I thought about him telling me to stay with my team.   There he was, just days earlier "flirting with the angels," and now he's worried about me getting my team ready for a tournament.

Always stay close to the people you love and to those that love you. Always be there for the people that need you.

Lesson #14: Life Is Short. Live Every Day To Its Fullest

Dad recovered well enough from his 1998 incident to leave the hospital, but he never fully recovered. He could walk only very short distances, maybe 20 or 30 feet, with the help of a walker. Anything longer than that required the use of a wheelchair. It was that way until he suffered a series of debilitating strokes in 2001. By late 2001 he was unable to move his legs, had limited use of his arms, and was not able to speak. He was now confined to a hospital bed which had been moved into the living room of my parent's home.

With my Dad unable to speak, it meant our weekly phone calls had come to an end. It was a very strange feeling when the phone didn't ring as you expected it to, especially on Sunday mornings. A worse feeling was in knowing that even if I called home I wouldn't be able to speak with him. I also felt guilty because I had previously commented to my wife how Dad was developing a habit of repeating himself and telling me the same stories over and over again when we spoke on the phone. Now, facing the realization that Dad could no longer speak, I would have done anything to have just one more conversation with him. He could tell me the same things over and over again and it would have been perfectly fine with me, but it wasn't going to happen.

October 18, 2003 is a day my son, Cam, and I will remember forever, but for very different reasons. It was a Saturday and we were in South Bend, IN for the Notre Dame – USC football game. I had never been to a Notre Dame game and was really excited to be able to see them play USC. As a kid I always liked USC, but I think it was more because of their colors than anything else. They were red and gold, the same colors as my hometown Hancock Bulldogs. Cam was obviously very excited as well. Here was a 7-year-old boy about to see his first college football game and it involved his favorite team, the Notre Dame Fighting Irish. I still don't know how he developed such a strong allegiance to the 'Irish, but it probably had something to do with all the team hats, shirts, footballs, and foam fingers he was given by our good friends, Dave and Lynn Harvey. Their son, Scott, had attended law school at Notre Dame and was a big Irish football fan himself. I was never much of a Notre Dame fan, but I would be lying if I said I wasn't intrigued by their great football history and tradition. The Notre Dame Victory March, The Four Horsemen, Knute Rockne, Touchdown Jesus, the Gipper…..yes, it was going to be a day to remember.

We had great seats, the weather was perfect, mid-60's with plenty of sunshine, and I was living a "dream come true day" with my son. It was a good game, at least early on, as each team scored on their first possession and the first quarter ended with USC leading 21-14. Early in the second quarter, however, USC started to take control. Notre Dame decided they weren't going to drive the ball on offense nor tackle on defense and the game quickly turned into a laugher. In the end, USC quarterback Matt Leinart picked apart the 'Irish secondary, to the tune of 351 yards and four touchdowns, and lead the Trojans to a 45-14 victory.

It would not have been right for me to pass on the opportunity to take an "all in good fun" shot at Cam's beloved Irish on the way back to the car.

"Maybe if your defense would tackle someone once in a while you'd have a better chance of winning," I said, pulling his Notre Dame hat down over his eyes as we worked our way down the crowded walkway.

"Yeah, well, if Matt Leinart wasn't your quarterback you guys wouldn't have won today!" he shot back, adjusting his hat so he could see again.

After a 10 or 15 minute walk we were back in the car and Cam used my cell phone to Call his Mom. She had passed on the game, opting for the South Bend mall instead. Cam told her we were on our way and would be at the mall in a few minutes. We picked her up, grabbed some food at the

Burger King drive through, and headed for Traverse City. We were only 30 minutes or so out of South Bend when my cell phone rang.

"Hello?" I said.

"Chris, this is Greg." It was my brother and I could tell immediately something was wrong.

"What's going on?" I asked.

"They took Dad to the hospital," he said. "He's really sick and…….." his voice trailed off. A few moments passed and a new voice came on the phone. It was Greg's wife, Wanda.

"Hi," she said.

"What happened?" I asked.

"Your Dad started coughing really hard and then his breathing got really shallow," Wanda explained.

"Your Mom called the ambulance and they rushed him to the hospital," she added.

"How bad is he?" I asked.

Wanda was an ER nurse herself and often helped my Mom take care of Dad in their home. I knew of all people she would have a pretty good idea of my Dad's true condition.

"I'm not going to lie to you," she said. "He's in pretty bad shape. I honestly don't think he's going to make it."

"Well I'm on my way back from Indiana, but I'll get there as soon as I can," I said and hung up.

"Your Dad?" asked my wife.

"Yeah, this time it sounds really bad," I said with tears coming to my eyes. "I just hope he can hang on until I get there."

Another 30 minutes or so passed and my phone rang again. This time it was my Mom.

"Hi Chris," she said.

"Hi Mom. How are you doing?" I asked.

"You heard, huh? Somebody called you?" she asked.

"Yeah, I talked to Greg and Wanda a little while ago," I told her. "Wanda said he's not doing well."

"No, he's not doing well at all," my Mom said. "You need to come home."

This was very different from the incident in 1998. My Mom, at that time, was playing it cool, not wanting me to worry so she didn't give any more details than she needed to. This time, however, things were different. My Dad's condition was very serious and she wasn't trying to hide it. Her voice was strong, but you could tell she was sad. Like she knew the end was near. I needed to come home. I have an older sister and three younger brothers, all of whom still live in Hancock. They were there, I was not, and I got a terribly sick feeling in my stomach just thinking about it.

*If he dies before I get there...*I thought. I was a four-hour drive from Traverse City and then still had another seven hours to go from there. *That's a lot of time for things to go wrong...*

We got back to Traverse City just before 11 p.m. My wife and I decided on the drive home that it would be best for her and Cam to stay in Traverse City. She had to work, Cam had to go to school, and there was no telling how long I would be gone. I quickly threw together a duffel bag with some clothes and overnight necessities and started my long drive to Hancock.

For almost the whole trip I kept saying the same thing over and over again. *Please Dad, just don't go before I get there. Please....*

That drive is long no matter which way you go and what time of year it is, but when you feel like you're racing against the clock it makes the trip even longer. I pulled in to Hancock just after 7 a.m. and drove straight to the hospital. I wondered if the hospital staff would allow me in to my Dad's room that early, but when I got there nobody was around and so I headed straight for his room. I pushed the door open and saw him lying in bed. My Mom was in a chair next to him. She looked up when she heard the door swing open.

"You made it," she said.

"Yeah, it was a long drive, but I'm here…finally," I said.

It was now Sunday morning and my Mom hadn't left my Dad's side since he was taken to the hospital the day before. Surprisingly to me she didn't look at all tired. Her eyes just looked very, very sad. It was just my Mom and I. We watched my Dad laying there seemingly fighting to breathe. It was almost like it took every ounce of energy he had just to take a breath. Each breath was very slow, very deep, and he looked very uncomfortable. He was sweating profusely, his eyes barely open, and my Mom kept dabbing his forehead with a wash cloth to keep the sweat from running down his face.

I sat down in a chair near the window, put my elbows on my knees, and rested my chin in my hands. I continued to watch my Mom wipe my Dad's forehead and I noticed that it now looked like my Dad was staring back at my Mom even though his eyes were still barely open. I wondered what he was thinking, or if he was thinking at all, and I started to cry.

"Why are you crying?" my Mom asked.

"This is just so damn unfair," I said.

"Why do you say that?" she asked.

"I watched you and Dad work so hard for so long. Then he gets sick, can't do anything, and you end up not being able to do anything either because you have to take care of him. Now look at him." I said, starting to cry harder with each word.

"You guys deserved to have a great retirement together and this is what you get?" I said. "It's not fair."

"Oh, we had a couple of good years there," my Mom said referring to the little time they did have to enjoy retirement together. "Dad wouldn't want you talking about that."

Each day was basically the same. We would read, talk, and just be there with my Dad. I would stay for most of the day, leaving for an hour or so to get something to eat, and then

I would spend the night at my parents' house, which was the same house in which I grew up. When morning came I would drive back to the hospital and our daily routine would begin again.

On Wednesday, after watching my Dad struggle for the better part of four days, I stood next to him and suddenly felt the urge to speak.

"Dad," I said. "It sure seems like you're having a tough time. I want you to know that if you want to leave us now, it's OK, we'll understand."

I rubbed my hand on his forehead, just like he had always done to me when I was sick as a young boy. I remembered how comforting it was when he did that and hoped that he felt the same comfort now. There was no reaction from my Dad, but all I could do was just hope that he heard me.

Thursday, after spending most of the day at the hospital, I ended up falling asleep on the couch in my parent's living room. I was suddenly awakened by the phone ringing and took a quick glance at the clock. It was 12:30 a.m. No call at that time of day is ever good. It was my brother, Greg.

"Hello?" I said.

"Hey, it's Greg," he said. "The hospital just called.....Dad died. We're all going back to the hospital right now."

"OK," I answered.

I hung up the phone just as my sister was opening the door to an upstairs bedroom.

"Is it Dad?" she asked.

"Yeah," I replied. "He died a few minutes ago. We need to go back to the hospital."

I got into my car, went to start the engine, then stopped and leaned back against the seat.

It's over, I thought. *I can't believe he's gone.*

Back at the hospital the parking lot was virtually empty. Looking from the outside there were no lights visible in any of the rooms. It was dark, very quiet, and kind of eerie yet peaceful at the same time. Because of the early hour, the main doors were locked so I was directed to an entrance in the back. After making my way through a maize of doors, hallways, and stairs I came to my Dad's room. As I pushed open the door I saw all of my brothers, their wives, my sister, and my Mom. There were no lights on in the room except one very dim light directly above my Dad's bed. He was lying there, now completely still. No more struggling to breathe, no more sweating, no more fighting to stay alive. He was at peace now and looked more comfortable than he had in a very long time. We all sat in his room together and Mom told us how he went quietly and just stopped breathing. She told us how her worst fear was that he wouldn't be able to go peacefully.

We stayed for almost an hour and Mom decided it was time for us all to go home. She was sitting in the chair next to Dad's bed, the same spot she had been in since Sunday, and she stood up to leave. Stepping close to my Dad she looked down at him and started to cry. She bent over, kissed him on the forehead and laid her head down on the pillow next to his. It was heart wrenching to say the least. She stayed that way for a few seconds then stood up, wiped the tears from her face, and walked out of the room. My brothers, sister, and sister-in-laws followed her while I stayed behind. I needed a few moments alone with my Dad. I stood close, bent over and kissed his cheek, and rubbed his forehead one last time. Then I spoke to him.

"Dad," I said. "I'm really sorry things turned out this way. You deserved so much better. You really did. I appreciate everything you did for me and for all that you taught me along the way. I love you, Dad. I'm going to miss you."

I knew the day would come when my Dad was no longer here. As much as I thought I was well prepared for that day, the truth is you really can't prepare yourself. The finality of it all is just not something you can prepare for. I still really miss him even though it's been almost five years since he passed away. However, I also feel very blessed to have had such a great relationship with him. A relationship full of laughs, lessons, opportunities, and once-in-a-lifetime memories. His spirit remains alive and I pray I will be able to walk with him again some day.

Life is very short. Too short to spend precious time worrying about things that aren't important and circumstances you can't control. Instead, spend your time living life to its fullest, every single day, and cherish each minute you have with those you care about. Tell them you love them and tell them today. If you wait until tomorrow it may be too late.

EPILOGUE

Attending my Dad's visitation and funeral were two of the more difficult things I've had to do in my lifetime. However, at the same time, both events gave me an opportunity to speak with others about the impact my Dad had on their lives. It seemed they all had comments with a recurring theme. That being, how he had such a kind heart and always made them feel like they were the most important person in his life even though, they said, everyone knew the most important people in his life were his wife and children. Never at a loss for a joke or funny story my Dad had a way of making sure every conversation he had ended with smiles all around. If you were a friend of his, and he had many, you knew he would do anything for you and could be counted on whenever and wherever you needed him.

Since his passing I have talked to several of his former Little League baseball players. Now grown men, with wives and children of their own, each one spoke of the positive influence he had on their lives. They said they appreciated how he treated them not like kids, but rather, like young men. Accepting each one with their individual strengths and weaknesses then molding them into one cohesive unit. He didn't coach in hope that someday he would churn out the next great major league baseball player. Instead, he took the sport he loved and used it to help teach young boys life lessons that would help them grow up to be great people.

A family friend summarized my Dad's life this way, "With a twinkle in his eye, a smile on his face, constant words of encouragement, and a heart that only knew how to give, Bill Givens made this world a better place. His life was a wonderful example of the positive impact one person can make. He will be missed, but his legacy lives on in his family, friends, and community he loved."

Printed in the United States
214882BV00001B/13/P